Summary
of

Thank You for Being Late
Thomas L. Friedman

Conversation Starters

By BookHabits

Please Note: This is an unofficial conversation starters guide. If you have not yet read the original work, please do so first. Buy the book here.

We hope you enjoy this complementary guide from BookHabits. Our mission is to aid readers and reading groups with quality, thought provoking material to in the discovery and discussions on some of today's favorite books.

Tips for Using BookHabits Conversation Starters:

EVERY GOOD BOOK CONTAINS A WORLD FAR DEEPER THAN the surface of its pages. The characters and their world come alive through the words on the pages, yet the characters and its world still live on. Questions herein are designed to bring us beneath the surface of the page and invite us into the world that lives on. These questions can be used to:

- Foster a deeper understanding of the book
- Promote an atmosphere of discussion for groups
- Assist in the study of the book, either individually or corporately
- Explore unseen realms of the book as never seen before

About Us:

THROUGH YEARS OF EXPERIENCE AND FIELD EXPERTISE, from newspaper featured book clubs to local library chapters, *BookHabits* can bring your book discussion to life. Host your book party as we discuss some of today's most widely read books.

Table of Contents

Introducing *Thank You for Being Late*

THREE-TIME PULITZER WINNER AND *NEW YORK TIMES* foreign affairs columnist Thomas L. Friedman expresses a sense of urgency in the need to understand the interacting forces of technology, global markets and climate change that make a complicated and threatening world we live in. These forces have resulted to accelerated changes, with a dizzying effect, and we need to know how to cope. In *Thank You For Being Late: An Optimist's Guide to Thriving in the Age of Accelerations,* the author explains how such forces are causing so much disruption and dislocation. We see loss of jobs and the ensuing anger and discontent among those affected even as wealth is created in other parts of the globe. The internet and global economies create opportunities but make international terrorism possible. These and many more are happening at the same time and even more rapidly than before.

Friedman emphasizes the need for knowledge and understanding. He said democracy can only work if voters are aware and informed. They can only make intelligent decisions on policy, for example, if they have an understanding of the real issues. The book aims to make readers aware of the complexities involved in the fast-changing developments in the 21st century because their lives are affected in many ways: their jobs are threatened, their environments become unlivable, species go extinct while carbon levels increase, governments are even more ineffective.

Before his data-driven explanations however, he tells the engaging story of his friendship with Bojia, an Ethiopian political exile in the US who works as a parking attendant by day and a blogger at night. Bojia shared his immigrant experience and his goal to inform people of political issues plaguing Ethiopia through his blog. Friedman in turn shared his writing skills as a columnist. Their conversation highlighted how local and national issues have become a global discussion. Friedman gives the readers a short course on how he writes his columns and what a columnist's goal is. He then goes back to his initial idea by saying that what is important is that the columnist should be constantly learning to keep abreast in a fast-changing world.

Friedman gives deeply researched examples of dislocation happening in different parts of the world and how these are results of technological, environmental and economic fast-paced developments. In coping with what he calls the "age of acceleration" he proposes that people and governments should: be quick to adapt and be innovative; help those who have a hard time adjusting to change; and able to slow down to think and stay connected to ones values. He identified 18 steps to face the challenges. Some of these include free-trade deals, corporate tax cuts, sugar ban, building infrastructure, expansion of adult learning programs, tighter border controls, and setting up a single-payer healthy system. Friedman also stressed that people and governments can learn from Mother Nature's examples and lessons about sustainability, adaptability and interdependence.

He makes an important suggestion about nurturing community values. He said strong communities can help solve the challenges to acceleration. To make us understand, he tours us to his own childhood community in Minneapolis where the style of government has become inclusive and harmonious. In the years when his family lived in that neighborhood, democratic processes worked well and the economy helped families achieve middle class status. Friedman is positive that communities like these are the solution to 21st century dislocation.

Friedman quotes a lot of resource persons, many of them leaders in the technology and business fields. This is his "radically inclusive" approach --to consider as many relevant people, organizations, disciplines, processes and technologies. This reflects the kind of thinking he suggests in order to comprehend the complex world we are in. The book is full of metaphors and catchy slogans that hope to illustrate his points. He has a light tone and often times uses humor to lighten the effect of absorbing and connecting so many facts, figures and ideas.

Thank You For Being Late is the seventh and reportedly his most ambitious work. It is a *New York Times* bestseller, currently on its seventh week in the list as of June 17, 2017. Though it has reviewers who praised the book's merits, the book is also disliked by other reviewers who criticized the folksy writing style, its repetitiveness, and its use of rehashed ideas taken from the author's previous columns and books. Friedman's fame as a writer started with his first book *From Beirut to Jerusalem* which won the 1989 National Book Award for nonfiction and the 1989 Overseas Press Club Award for the best book on foreign policy. It stayed on the *New York Times* bestseller list for almost 12 months. The six books that followed, including this latest one, also achieved bestseller status.

Introducing the Author

THOMAS L. FRIEDMAN IS THE BESTSELLING AUTHOR OF multiple books and an award-winning journalist who won the Pulitzer Prize three times for reporting and commentary on international issues.

His first book, *From Beirut to Jerusalem,* published in 1989, was about the developments in Lebanon and Israel during the 1980s when Israel invaded Lebanon and the first Palestinian intifada erupted. The book became a bestseller in The *New York Times* list for almost 12 months, and won two awards: the 1989 National Book Award for nonfiction and the 1989 Overseas Press Club Award. His second book, *The Lexus and the Olive Tree* was published in 1999. He argued in this book that the changing face of international relations could best be understood as an interaction of old forces and the new. Globalization, referring to the trade and finance between nations, has replaced the Cold War. The old forces of nationalism and ethnicity were sometimes checked by the forces of globalization, but sometimes they were more powerful. Friedman suggested that leaders of nations ought to understand such interactions if they were to be effective in office.

Friedman's columns for the *New York Times* discussed issues related to the bombing of the World Trade Center on 9/11. The collection of commentaries was published as the book *Longitudes and Attitudes.* Among the most controversial commentaries he wrote were those that supported President George W. Bush in his war against Iraq. Looking back at those difficult times, Friedman later admitted that it was a mistake to support the US intervention in Iraq. He was in a hurry to see democracy and pluralism installed, but realized that it cannot be hurried; the cost of the conflict was too high.

Globalization became an even more urgent issue in few years time after he wrote his second book. Friedman realized that he needed to update many of the globalization stories he earlier wrote, thus, in 2005 he came out with his fourth book *The World is Flat.* The book achieved the #1 bestseller in the *New York Times* list became the Financial Times/Goldman Sachs Business Book of the Year Award in 2005. In 2008, *Hot, Flat, and Crowded* published. Friedman wrote the book to stress the need for nation-building in America. Institutions have not been effective—Washington, public schools, infrastructure, among others. The biggest challenge for the country is how to face the planet's environmental degradation. He suggested that America take the lead in creating clean technologies.

His sixth book, *That Used to Be Us was released in* 2011. Co-authored with Michael Mendelbaum, the book suggested steps to be taken to sustain the American dream and remain a world power. *Thank You For Being Late* is Friedman's latest book, his seventh bestseller in the *New York Times* list.

Friedman started his journalism career as a London reporter and later on as Beirut correspondent for United Press International (UPI) in 1979. He joined the staff of The *New York Times* in 1981 as financial reporter tackling OPEC and oil-related issues. He became Beirut Bureau Chief in 1982 covering the events that followed the Israeli invasion of Lebanon. As Jerusalem Bureau Chief in 1984 he reported on West Bank and Gaza developments that led to the first Palestinian intifada that gave him the topic for his first book. From 1989 to 1995, he worked as Chief Diplomatic Correspondent in Washington, D.C., Chief White House Correspondent, International Economic

Correspondent, and the Foreign Affairs columnist which he occupies currently.

He won Pulitzer Prizes for: 1983 international reporting (from Lebanon), 1988 international reporting (from Israel), and 2002 distinguished commentary.

As a young boy, Friedman wanted to be a professional golfer and played in various tournaments. It was however his passion for journalism introduced to him by his high school teacher Hattie Steinberg that inspired him for life.

Discussion Questions

"Get Ready to Enter a New World"

Tip: Begin with questions dealing with broader issues to ensure ample time for quality discussions. Read through all discussion questions before engaging.

~ ~ ~

question 1

Thomas L. Friedman wrote the book because he wanted to help readers better understand the many changes taking place in the world today. Changes are happening at such a fast pace that people need to stay informed in order to be able to make proper decisions that concern society, he said. Being informed well prevents people from becoming victims of false teachers, religious and ideological fanatics, and people who try to deliberately mislead others. Do you agree that learning and understanding are essential for the health of society? Does it make you a better citizen if you are well-informed?

~ ~ ~

~ ~ ~

question 2

Three major forces - technology, globalization, and climate change-- are making fast changes in societies, workplaces, and communities according to Friedman. Can you cite changes happening in your community, school or workplace that are fast changing? Are these connected to technology, globalization, and climate change?

~ ~ ~

~~~

question 3

He calls himself an explanatory journalist, one who translates
"English to English". His previous best-selling books explained
complicated topics like globalization and climate change. Do you
think his current book gave clear and understandable account of
why the world is speeding up and getting complicated? Can you
cite an example of how he explained a complex theme?

~~~

~ ~ ~

question 4

People have been feeling the results of technological shifts. For example the manual way of milking cows has given way to digitized methods and has dislocated farm workers. Friedman says the computerization of human jobs is speeding up the world in many other ways causing a radical disruption of lives and systems. People are feeling dislocated. Have you seen people being dislocated because of digitization of work? How have they reacted to the change? Are there changes like these in your community?

~ ~ ~

~~~

question 5

The author cited his hometown of Minneapolis as an example of how communities can solve the problem of change and acceleration. Communities that practice democratic ideals and address economic problems can effectively respond to the challenges. He suggested that strengthening of communities. Do you agree that communities can help solve the challenge of acceleration? Is your own community effectively addressing the social and economic needs of its residents?

~~~

~ ~ ~

question 6

The author used data gathered from travels, interviews with authorities in the field, conversations with the common man to write the book. He often quotes leaders in business and technology to explain his points. His conversations with a parking attendant is recounted. Do you think these are good ways to gather information? Would you do them if you are writing your own book?

~ ~ ~

~~~

question 7

The title of the book is inspired by Friedman's moments of being alone and having time to think about important matters while waiting for people who are late for their appointments with him. He said he was always on a rush and the waiting gave him time to think about his writing projects. What can you say about the way he manages his time? Do you think it is a good way to write a book? Are there negative aspects to it?

~~~

~ ~ ~

question 8

He explains how technology is developing at so much speed and beyond what human brains can take. Friedman then suggests that new ways of thinking and doing that will have to be done in order to adapt to changes. He quoted an authority who said one should think without a box instead of thinking outside the box. He said this meant one has to be inclusive of all ideas, disciplines, people, processes, and many others in order to come up with solutions. Do you think "thinking without a box" is possible? Can you give an example of thinking without a box as compared to inside the box?

~ ~ ~

~ ~ ~

question 9

The author says the acceleration of the joint effects of technology, market forces, and climate change will continue and governments cannot do anything about it. He believes that people will be able to adjust as long as they work hard to accommodate and adjust to the changes. It can start with well-functioning communities. People will be able to achieve "dynamic stability." Do you agree with his optimism? Why? Why not?

~ ~ ~

~ ~ ~

question 10

Friedman explains that Mother Nature has shown lessons that humans can learn in order to adjust to change. The principles of sustainability, adaptability, and interdependence are practices that will help. Are you convinced by his explanations and examples about Mother Nature? Why? Why not?

~ ~ ~

~~~

question 11

Friedman told the story of Bojia at the start of the book. Bojia is an Ethiopian who sought asylum in the US because his government did not favor his political activities. He writes a blog that informs people of the political situation in Ethiopia, but he is also works as a parking attendant to pay his bills. Why do you think Friedman put his story at the beginning of the book? Do you think this is a good way to illustrate the confluence of technology and problems in developing countries?

~~~

~ ~ ~

question 12

Friedman used catchy slogans like "build floors, not walls" and "turning AI into IA" to make his writing more interesting. These were written alongside data-driven explanations about technology and climate change. Do you think this is a good way to make the reading lighter? What effect do the slogans have on you as a reader?

~ ~ ~

~~~

question 13

Friedman stresses that humans are highly adaptable to change
and this makes him optimistic that people can face the challenge
of acceleration. His 18 suggestions to cope include building
infrastructure and passing free-trade deals. Do you think these
will be accomplished fast enough alongside the acceleration
that's already happening? Can humans implement these
solutions to match the pace of digital technology?

~~~

~ ~ ~

question 14

Friedman gives examples of how globalization and technology
forces interact and complicate each other. He cites climate
change in Niger which is causing farms to dry up, even as
technology is prolonging children's lives, leading to a hungry
population of 72 million by 2050. Can you cite other examples of
acceleration and its complications? Are his examples clear and
convincing? Do figures help you understand?

~ ~ ~

~~~

question 15

One way of explaining acceleration that the author did was to point out how big and fast the internet is. He said 10 billion things are connected to it, but this is just less than 1 percent of the possible. Many more things like cars, bodies, gadgets are joining every day. What things have you added to the internet recently? What other things are you planning to add in the future? Can you imagine what the author is trying to say?

~~~

~~~

question 16

The book is on its seventh week as bestseller in the *New York Times* list as of third week of June 2017. Despite critics who dislike his writing style, readers continue to buy Friedman's books. Why do you think he continues to land on the bestseller list?

~~~

~~~

question 17

Friedman's writing has been described by Goodreads and *Slate* reviewers as folksy, ostentatious, and over-simplistic. They say that his style has gotten worse in his latest book and is full of "incongruous punchy asides." Do you think this is a valid comment of his book? Why? Why not?

~~~

~ ~ ~

question 18

Slate reviewer Justin Peters thinks that Friedman is merely forwarding the interests of business and technology developers. Instead of regulating technology and globalization, Friedman is reportedly suggesting people to "roll with the changes" and remake institutions to accommodate change and flow. This means that labor unions, government regulation, progressive populism and other efforts that help protect the welfare and rights of the poor and majority are not given much importance. Do you agree with the review? Does the reviewer have important points we should consider?

~ ~ ~

~ ~ ~

question 19

Friedman's description of his trip back to St. Louis Park where he grew up is called by the *New York Times* review as the "most elegiac, memorable part of the book". He recounted the good memories he had there. He also discussed communal virtues that it had that serve as examples for other communities. Do you agree that that part of the book is the most elegiac and memorable?

~ ~ ~

~~~

question 20

This is Friedman's seventh book. His other books hit the bestseller list with topics that discussed the Middle East wars, globalization, and America as a world leader. Why do you think readers like to read his ideas on these topics? What most interested you in the book? Will you read his other books after reading this one?

~~~

~ ~ ~

question 21

Friedman grew up in St. Louis Park, a middle-class suburb in Minneapolis, Minnesota. He takes readers back to his childhood neighborhood to cite an example of how a democratic and economically sustainable community can be the solution to global acceleration. Do you think your communities are good examples of strong and well- functioning communities that Friedman is upholding? Will your communities support its residents to face the effects of acceleration?

~ ~ ~

~ ~ ~

question 22

Friedman is optimistic that the US and other nations would be able to deal with the challenge of accelerations. In recent years however, the threat of internet and technology-assisted terrorism has been accelerating too. How feasible is Friedman's optimism do you think? Can his 18 suggestions a fast enough solution to stave off international terrorism?

~ ~ ~

~ ~ ~

question 23

The title of the book refers to Friedman's need to slow down to have time to think more clearly and connect to one's values. He said it is an important habit in this age of acceleration. Do you think he is correct? Do you feel the need to slow down too in order to think about important matters that concern you?

~ ~ ~

~ ~ ~

question 24

Bojia, Friedman's Ethiopian friend, came to the US for political asylum. He writes a blog to advocate Ethiopian political issues and works as a parking attendant by day. Do you think Bojia and his blog is a good example of how internet technology provides solutions for developing countries that are not fully democratic? Do you think Ethiopian politics and its justice system will "accelerate" for the better because of blogs like his?

~ ~ ~

~ ~ ~

question 25

Friedman learned journalism from Hattie Steinberg, his high school teacher who inspired him to be a reporter. She stressed the importance of quality work and to act professionally. She taught at a time when there was no internet. Do you think her lessons still apply today when the internet has changed and accelerated journalism methods?

~ ~ ~

~~~

question 26

Friedman had years of experience as a journalist and foreign correspondent before he came out with his first book From Beirut to Jerusalem. He was on the field in Lebanon and Israel where he wrote reports for The *New York Times* and for which he won his Pulitzer Prizes. If he was assigned to other countries instead, in South Asia or Australia for example, would he have published a bestselling book just the same? Why? Why not?

~~~

~ ~ ~

question 27

Hattie Steinberg, Friedman's journalism teacher in high school, inspired him to pursue journalism as a career. She demanded high journalistic standards from her students. If Friedman had another teacher, would he have been inspired to pursue journalism later in life?

~ ~ ~

~ ~ ~

question 28

Friedman traveled to places to gather information and file reports for the *New York Times*. In this age of the internet, people can report events from their own communities using their own cameras. How would Friedman's work be different if the internet existed during his time? Do you think he would have traveled as much and often?

~ ~ ~

~~~

question 29

Friedman's initial plan was to become a professional golf player.
His father inspired him to play the sport. If he pursued golf
instead, do you think he would have been just as successful?
Why? Why not?

~~~

~ ~ ~

question 30

Friedman's style of writing had been criticized by readers and critics. They say he uses metaphors that don't make sense, his language is too folksy, and is repetitive. If he changed his style to something more formal or literary, do you think his books would still be bestsellers? Would they sell more or less?

~ ~ ~

~~~

question 31

Friedman admitted that *Thank You For Being Late* is his most personal book since From Beirut to Jerusalem. He shared personal stories about his childhood which made him recall a lot of memorable moments.

~~~

~ ~ ~

question 32

Friedman's childhood neighborhood, St. Louis Park, was also the home of other successful men-- the Coen brothers Joel and Ethan, Senator Al Franken, NFL football coach Marc Trestman. Most of them graduated from the local Hebrew school, St. Louis Park High School.

~ ~ ~

~~~

question 33

Friedman spent two and a half years researching his seventh and latest book. He interviewed all the main technologists not once but twice in order to make sure his facts are updated.

~~~

~~~

question 34

Friedman travel research on climate change brought him to
West Africa, through Niger and then France. His team tracked
African refugees who left their villages and farms made
inhabitable by climate change and population explosion.
Without work and income, the refugees are flocking to Europe.

~~~

~ ~ ~

question 35

The first story Friedman published as a high school reporter was
his story on the Israeli general Ariel Sharon who was a hero in
the Six-Day War. He covered his lecture at the University of
Minnesota and interviewed him.

~ ~ ~

~~~

question 36

Friedman did not immediately land as reporter for his high school paper. Hattie Steinberg, his journalism teacher, thought he was not yet good enough, so she made him the paper's business manager. He sold ads to local pizza parlors.

~~~

~~~

question 37

As a foreign correspondent for UPI in Beirut from 1979 to 1981, Friedman was a multitasker-- file pictures and breaking news stories, do radio spots, even while ducking for cover. He said it was the best journalism school.

~~~

~ ~ ~

question 38

Apart from writing books and columns, Friedman made six
documentaries from 2003 to 2007 for the *New York Times*-
Discovery Channel joint project. Social, political and global issues
were featured in the documentaries.

~ ~ ~

Quiz Questions

"Ready to Announce the Winners?"

Tip: Create a leaderboard and track scores to see who gets the most correct answers. Winners required. Prizes optional.

~~~

quiz question 1

The three major forces of _____ are speeding up and changing workplaces, communities and societies, according to Friedman. The interaction of these three pose challenges that nations and governments will have to face.

~~~

~ ~ ~

quiz question 2

True or False: People need to understand the accelerations happening in the world in order to be able to make proper decisions. Friedman wrote *Thank You For Being Late* to help people understand the accelerations and the challenges involved.

~ ~ ~

~ ~ ~

quiz question 3

Friedman believes that _____ can help people face the challenges of acceleration. The practices of democratic processes and economic sustainability will strengthen these.

~ ~ ~

~~~

quiz question 4

Friedman grew up in _____in Minneapolis. He cites his neighborhood as a good example of a community that supports people to face challenges of acceleration.

~~~

~~~

quiz question 5

True or False: The title of the book was inspired by Friedman's disappointment when people come late for their appointments. He does not like waiting and of wasting time.

~~~

~~~

quiz question 6

The author is optimistic that people and nations can face the challenges posed by acceleration. He proposed 18 ways to make the adjustments.

~~~

~ ~ ~

quiz question 7

Friedman thinks people can learn from Mother Nature to face the challenge of acceleration. We can use the principles of sustainability, adaptability and interdependence to guide us.

~ ~ ~

~ ~ ~

quiz question 8

Thomas L. Friedman won the _____ for international reporting in 1983 and 1988, and for distinguished commentary in 2002. His first two awards were due to his coverage of Israeli invasion of Palestine and the Palestinian intifada. His distinguished commentary award is due to his columns about the Western and Muslim conflict after the bombing of the World Trade Center.

~ ~ ~

~~~

quiz question 9

True or False: The World is Flat is Friedman's first book. It discussed the issues and events behind the Israel - Palestine conflict in the 1980s.

~~~

~ ~ ~

quiz question 10

Friedman interviewed Saudi Arabia Crown Prince Abdullah bin Abdul Aziz in 2002 where he proposed his Arab-Israeli peace plan. He believes that despite its failure to be adopted by Israel and the US, the peace plan is the only true pan-Arab peace plan.

~ ~ ~

~ ~ ~

quiz question 11

Bojia, Friedman's blogger friend saought political asylum in the US. He works as a parking attendant. He is from _____.

~ ~ ~

~ ~ ~

quiz question 12

Friedman's high school journalism teacher was _____.
She stressed the importance of quality work and
professionalism.

~ ~ ~

Quiz Answers

1. Technology, globalization, climate change
2. True
3. Communities
4. St. Louis Park
5. False
6. True
7. True
8. Pulitzer Prize
9. False
10. True
11. Ethiopia
12. Hattie Steinberg

Ways to Continue Your Reading

EVERY month, our team runs through a wide selection of books to pick the best titles for readers and reading groups, and promotes these titles to our thousands of readers – sometimes with free downloads, sale dates, and additional brochures.

Want to register yourself or a book group? It's free and takes 1-click.

Register here.

On the Next Page...

Please write us your reviews! Any length would be fine but we'd appreciate hearing you more! We'd be SO grateful.

Till next time,

BookHabits

"Loving Books is Actually a Habit"

Made in the USA
Columbia, SC
17 December 2023

28783208R00039